To

FINANCIAL FREEDOM

Participant Portfolio

Written in collaboration with Progressive Bridges, Inc., 2015

From Paychecks To Power: 7 Power Moves To Finaancial Freedom Participant Portfolio
ISBN-978-0-9961303-1-8

This Product is designed to provide information in regard to the subject matter covered. It is sold with the understanding that the publisher is not engaged in rendering nor is responsible for legal or accounting services. If legal, accounting or industry specific advice is required, the services of a competent professional in those areas should be sought.

To purchase bulk orders or wholesale pricing visit website www.truefinancialcoaches.com and contact True Financial Coaches for more details and pricing.

7 POWER MOVES to FINANCIAL FREEDOM

Table of Contents

7 POWER MOVES *to* FINANCIAL FREEDOM

Participant Portfolio

Introduction:

The Participant Portfolio includes activities designed to promote engagement with the *From Paychecks to Power* text and help students and adults apply new financial knowledge in all areas of their lives.

Every portfolio lesson begins with a **Lesson Focus** to ensure primary lesson points. Specific lesson vocabulary is introduced in the **Financial Vocabulary** section prior to the lesson content, providing learners with some background knowledge of essential concepts included in the lesson. Students can complete the vocabulary activities independently within the portfolio.

The Participant Portfolio also includes a **variety of participant assessments** including a pre and post assessment, a checklist, and a financial decisions rubric.

A **Pre and Post Assessment**, a simple method of measuring growth of participant knowledge throughout the program. Answers are contained on the final page of this portfolio so that you can check your own growth.

The **7 POWER MOVES Checklist** can be made available for daily use as a self-assessment and/or teacher assessment throughout the program. Participants can view at a glance the financial behaviors that are needed for success in managing their personal finances. Having participants complete the checklist builds self-awareness, self-esteem, and growth on their journey to financial freedom.

The **7 POWER MOVES Rubric** is available for daily use by participants with persistent financial behavior challenges. Participants can rate their own exhibition of proactive financial behaviors and measure over time the increase in these behaviors as they develop new financially healthy habits.

A **College & Career Readiness checklist** is also included in the Participant Portfolio to support students with skills they need to master for success in the workplace. Shaded items within the checklist are contained within the *From Paychecks to Power* curriculum.

7 POWER MOVES *to* FINANCIAL FREEDOM

Best Practices in Financial Vocabulary Acquisition

Having trouble learning the financial terms? Use these activities on your own to help you understand and remember the meaning of the financial vocabulary.

1) **Vocabulary Note Cards**: In the four corners of the page, place the following information: The word and examples of the word. The meaning of the word in science, social studies, literature, or math. Why is this word important to know? The last corner create a sentence using that word.

2) **Quizlet Vocabulary Practice:** Download the Quizlet app onto your smart phone or tablet. Within the program, create vocabulary flashcards with the vocabulary in the chapter, including word meanings. Practice them daily through a variety of games within the app.

3) **Vocabulary Word Sort**: Divide the words in the list according to their part of speech. Resort the words into groups of words or concepts that go together based on word meanings.

4) **The Frayer Model**: Divide the paper into fourths. Write a vocabulary word in the center (or the intersection of both lines). In one corner, place your own definition of the word. In the second corner place facts or characteristics of the vocabulary word. In the third, place examples of the word, and in the fourth, place non-examples of the word. (http://www.longwood.edu/staff/jonescd/projects/educ530/aboxley/graphicorg/fraym.htm)

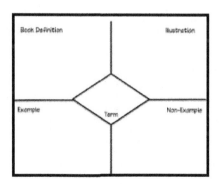

FROM PAYCHECKS TO POWER

Pre Test

What do you know about money and financial literacy? Do your best to complete each question. A pre/post assessment is a good way to review a book. It will give you an idea of how much information you have gained.

1. The wealthiest nation in the world is:

    a. China

    b. Iran

    c. United States of America

    d. Germany

2. The path to financial excellence/wealth is

    a. Finding the right investment to grow my investment quickly

    b. Hard work and discipline

    c. Meeting the right people and making the right connections

    d. Making the right deal

3. The best way to "get rich quick" is

    a. Find the right deal

    b. Borrow money to invest in a high yield account

    c. Don't

    d. Participate in a Nigerian scheme

4. Debt takes a toll on _____.

    a. Your ability to set-up an emergency fund

    b. Relationships

    c. Your health

    d. All of the above

5. Financial freedom is essentially about

    a. Writing a budget

    b. Personal behavior

    c. Calculating your expenses properly (Doing the math)

    d. How much money you make

6. Most Americans

    a. Have adequate funds in the bank to handle emergencies

    b. Live paycheck to paycheck

    c. Teach their children good financial habits through example

    d. Teach their children good financial habits intentionally

7. Personal finance is about

    a. How you handle your money

    b. Preparing a budget

    c. Managing your credit card balances properly

    d. Maintaining a good credit score

8. A borrower is

    a. Able to get what he wants when he wants it

    b. To be admired for his ability to get more credit

    c. Helping the economy by spending money

    d. A slave to the lender

9. The two major types of financial personalities are

    a. Saver and Spender

    b. Frugal and Spendthrift

    c. Free Spirit and Nerd

    d. Not easily defined

10. In planning a budget, it is important to know

    a.   What your parents thought about money

    b.   Your debt tolerance

    c.   Your Credit Score

    d.   Your financial personality

11. In order to make the sacrifices required for financial freedom, it is important to know the

    a.   Why

    b.   Amount

    c.   Bank Rate

    d.   Your Credit Score

12. Knowing why you are seeking financial freedom makes it easier to

    a.   Fail

    b.   Give up

    c.   Compromise

    d.   Keep going even when it gets tough

13. Our "financial kryptonite" is that one thing that

    a.   Keeps us focused on the goal

    b.   Derails our financial progress

    c.   Gives us real power

    d.   Enables us to get the goods we want now

14. Much advertising is based on

    a.   Appealing to our need to overcome low self-concept and self-image

    b.   A sincere desire to keep us well informed

    c.   Good intentions in helping us spend our money wisely

    d.   Keeping us up to date and current

15. Your credit score tells a lender

    a. Whether you can afford to make the payments required

    b. How good you are at borrowing money and paying it back

    c. Whether you manage your money well or not

    d. Whether you are a good provider for your family

16. Obtaining a mortgage to buy a house while not having a credit score, because you don't have a credit history, requires you to

    a. Build your credit first, so you have an extensive credit history

    b. Just accept that you can't afford to get a house

    c. Undergo "Manual Underwriting"

    d. Rely on friends or family to underwrite your mortgage

17. Which of the following are impossible to accomplish without a credit score

    a. Get a mobile (cell) phone account

    b. Buying a car

    c. Getting a job where the prospective employer pulls your credit history

    d. None of these, all are possible without a Credit Score

18. Statistically, when someone pays for items with cash they

    a. Spend less

    b. Spend more

    c. Spend the same

    d. Are happier with their purchase

19. One long-time, widely accepted, and highly successful method of budgeting is to use

    a. Credit cards, but always pay them off

    b. An envelope system and cash

    c. Separate checking accounts

    d. Your memory to inform you of whether a purchase is in your budget or not.

20. Being proactive means you are _____.

    a.   For everything

    b.   Exercise regularly

    c.   Fight hard for what is right

    d.   Intentional in your actions

21. A budget is

    a.   A tool used to achieve financial freedom

    b.   Denying access to things

    c.   Impossible to follow

    d.   By its very nature restrictive and difficult to stick to

22. Which type of budgeting is best for most people?

    a.   Open-Ended Budgeting

    b.   Zero-Based Budgeting

    c.   Both are equally beneficial for everyone

    d.   Neither, they are too restrictive

23. Household monthly budget meetings are necessary for

    a.   Reporting

    b.   Accountability

    c.   Maintenance of the budget

    d.   All of the above

24. Having a budget allows you to _____ your money.

    a.   Command

    b.   Spend

    c.   Save

    d.   Increase

25. Debt consolidation is not an effective way to get out of debt because

    a.   It doesn't get you out of owing the debt

    b.   The debt consolidator is the only one making money

    c.   It only treats the symptoms of the debt issue, not the cause

    d.   This is a false statement, because it is an effective solution

26. In using the "Debt Snowball" Method of getting out of debt, which would you pay first?

    a.   The debt with the lowest interest rate

    b.   The debt with the highest interest rate

    c.   The debt with the lowest balance

    d.   The debt with the highest balance

27. Integrity is

    a.   Being honest

    b.   Honoring your word

    c.   Having strong moral values

    d.   All of the above

28. What are the first bills that should be paid each month?

    a.   Clothing, food, transportation, insurance

    b.   Food, utilities, shelter, transportation

    c.   Food, cell phone, transportation, student loans

    d.   Credit cards, rent, food, clothes

29. A fully funded Emergency Fund will include how many months' worth of expenses

    a.   three to six

    b.   one to three

    c.   six to nine

    d.   nine to twelve

30. What is the recommended minimum down payment when purchasing a house?

   a.   5 percent

   b.   10 percent

   c.   20 percent

   d.   25 percent

31. If you must use a mortgage to buy a house, what is the recommended maximum term?

   a.   15-Year

   b.   20-year

   c.   30-Year

   d.   40-Year

32. What is the maximum percentage of your take home pay that should be allocated to a house payment in order for the payment to be considered affordable?

   a.   10

   b.   20

   c.   25

   d.   50

33. As a general rule of thumb, how much of your income should you invest?

   a.   15% of your take home from the very first paycheck

   b.   15% of your gross income from your very first paycheck

   c.   15% of your gross income, but only after you are debt-free and have a fully funded emergency-fund

   d.   Any excess income after paying your expenses

34. Practically speaking, the best retirement savings accounts are

   a.   Traditional IRAs, there is a reason they've been around a long time

   b.   Roth IRAs, these will grow tax free because you've already paid the taxes upfront

   c.   Savings Bonds

   d.   Bank Certificate of Deposits

35. Paying off your house using your discretionary income

    a.   Is a bad idea, because it eliminates the tax write off of mortgage interest

    b.   Is okay if you really want to

    c.   Puts you in the best position to build wealth

    d.   Just doesn't make sense, discretionary income is just for having fun and taking vacations

36. Someone who becomes debt-free by budgeting and managing their money becomes

    a.   financially powerful

    b.   financially responsible

    c.   financially independent

    d.   all of the above

POWER MOVES *to* FINANCIAL FREEDOM

For use with *From Paychecks to Power*

LESSON 1: INTRODUCTION

In the Wealthiest Nation in the World, Why are We SO Darn Broke?

Lesson Focus: The main focus of this lesson is to set the framework for the work that follows through an autobiographical account of the experiences of the author, setting himself apart as someone who has walked the walk on which the reader will now embark.

Read *From Paychecks to Power*, pgs. 9-12

Financial Vocabulary: financially responsible, creditor, debtor, living wage, salary (salaries), bank account, wealth, saving(s), economy, income, payments, money, personal finance, financial coach, prosper (prosperity), paycheck, paycheck to paycheck, financial goals

Use one of the vocabulary activities in the Best Practices in Financial Vocabulary Acquisition in the beginning of the book

Why is the average American broke? Use 3-5 vocabulary words in your answer.

_____

_____

_____

_____

In other countries such as France and Germany, citizens save at a rate of 5 times that of the United States. Why do you think citizens from other countries find it easier to save?

_____

_____

_____

Based on your reading so far, how would you rate your lifestyle? Fill in the Savings and Debt columns by shading from the bottom up according to your ratings.

RATING	SAVINGS	DEBT
FREEDOM 5	LARGE SAVINGS	NO DEBT
3	SOME SAVINGS	SOME DEBT
1	PAYCHECK TO PAYCHECK	HIGH AMOUNT OF DEBT

How do you make your buying decisions? List 3 criteria you use to determine whether or not you will buy something when you realize that you desire it.

1. _____

2. _____

3. _____

Where have you spent most of your money? Draw an item below that illustrates the answer to this question.

How do you spend your money?

What is the average amount of money available to you each week after necessary bills are paid?

_____

Place the amount you think you spend in each category below. Then track your actual spending for a week by writing every penny spent in the remaining columns. Add up your actual week to see how close you came to your estimate.

Spending Category	Weekly Spending Estimate	Actual Day 1	Actual Day 2	Actual Day 3	Actual Day 4	Actual Day 5	Actual Day 6	Actual Day 7	Total Actual Spending
Entertain.									
Transport.									
Food									
Education									
Clothing									
Personal Care									
Other									
Totals									

Reflection:

What did you notice about your daily spending habits?   Analyze the differences between your estimated and actual spending. Did anything surprise you? _____

_____
_____
_____
_____
_____
_____
_____
_____
_____
_____

Income, Savings & Debt History

Estimate and record your last 3 years of total income and debt. Add notes explaining reasons for the amounts.

Year	Estimated Total Income	Estimated Total Savings	Estimated Total Debt	Notes

Reflection:

Do you notice any trends over the last 3 years? Were the different amounts of savings and debt directly related to specific events? Explain your observations. _____

_____
_____
_____
_____

What is your current buying mantra? For example, for some people it might be, "I deserve this." Write it in the thought bubble.

Hunt for Habits of Financial Success:

Research the following 2 scenarios. Look for 4 financial habits of each person and record them in the appropriate areas below.

Scenario #1: Research someone who was wealthy & lost a lot of money. What were 4 habits enabled this decrease?

Scenario #2: Research someone who grew up in poverty. but overcame poverty to succeed financially. What were 4 habits that enabled this increase?

Negative Habits:

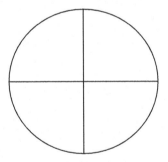

Positive Habits:

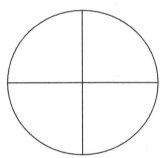

Rate Yourself:

The author states that making changes takes hard work. Rate your **desire** for change, as well as your **level of commitment** to the work required to make this change. Place an "X" on each continuum below that reflects your desire and level of commitment to this process.

Little Desire ⟷ **High Desire**

Low Commitment ⟷ **High Commitment**

FROM PAYCHECKS TO POWER Journal Entry

Consider your current thoughts, practices, habits, and experiences related to this chapter. Record your thoughts about them as you think about your successes, reflections, successes, hang-ups, and resolutions

Reflections:

_____

_____

Successes:

_____

_____

_____

Frustrations:

_____

_____

_____

Decisions:

_____

_____

_____

7 POWER MOVES *to* FINANCIAL FREEDOM

For use with *From Paychecks to Power*

LESSON 2: CHAPTER 1

A Journey to Broke and Back: My Story

Lesson Focus: The focus of this lesson is the telling of the author's personal journey onto debt and his journey back out. It reveals many of the causal events that lead to debt, but through example provides hope for a way out.

Read *From Paychecks to Power*, pgs. 13-26

Financial Vocabulary: personal finance, prosper, philosophy, principles, practices, financial management, choices, disposable income, Nigerian scheme, bank, cash, debt, debit card, credit card, check, financial responsibility, fraud, budget, bankruptcy, need, want, financial rehabilitation, credit union, financed, recession, identity theft, credit report, credit monitoring, consumer, payment, paycheck, paycheck to paycheck, emergency fund, debt snowball, financial empowerment, naïve, scam (scammed), CPA, declined (as in the credit card was declined)

*Use one of the vocabulary activities on page 6 if you struggle to remember Financial Vocabulary meanings.

Before & After:

The author describes himself before and after his financial transformation. List the vocabulary words that have to do with the author BEFORE his financial transformation in the BEFORE area. List the vocabulary words that have to do with the author AFTER his financial transformation in the AFTER area.

BEFORE	AFTER

Draw & label the contents of a financially successful person's wallet.

What are 3 things your parents taught you about money?

1. _____

2. _____

3. _____

The BEST way to get rich quick is _____.

How can you tell if you are living from paycheck to paycheck?

_____
_____
_____
_____
_____
_____
_____
_____
_____
_____

How did the author finally get himself out of debt? Complete each bubble with one action the author took to get himself out of debt.

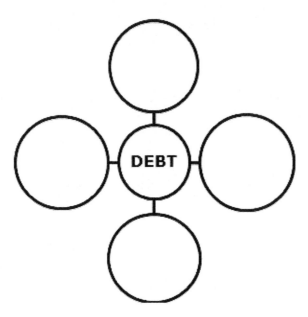

> *"When you get your finances in order, you will get your life in order."*
>
> **Shannaan Dawda**

Reflection:

What do you think the author means with this quote?

_____

_____

_____

Benefits of Living Debt Free:

List 3 benefits of living debt free experienced by the author.

1. _____

2. _____

3. _____

Eliminating Debt Scenario:

The author describes how the "debt snowball" works. Given the following circumstances, how would you position the following debts in a payoff plan? List your debt elimination plan below the table. After listing the steps of your plan, be sure to include justification for your choices.

Debt	Balance due	Interest Rate
Car loan	$8000	22%
Credit Card 1	$800	12%
Credit Card 2	$1300	25%
Bank loan	$3000	8%

Plan to Eliminate Debt:

Step #1 - _____

Step #2 - _____

Step #3 - _____

Step #4 - _____

How long do you think it would take to pay off the debt listed above if the borrower were to spend $500/month paying down the debt?

_____

What would you do to pay down the debt faster if you were the borrower? Why?

_____

_____

_____

_____

_____

My Passion:

The author was able to start his own meaningful business, his passion, because he was financially secure. What would you do if you were financially stable and had a good salary? Draw something to illustrate your passion.

Goals for Learning about Financial Freedom:

After hearing the author's own financial growth story, what are you looking forward to learning the most from his book?

_____

_____

_____

_____

List 3 goals you have now for your own financial situation.

1. _____

2. _____

3. _____

FROM PAYCHECKS TO POWER Journal Entry

Consider your current thoughts, practices, habits, and experiences related to this chapter. Record your thoughts about them as you think about your successes, reflections, successes, hangups, and resolutions

Reflections:

_____

_____

Successes:

_____

_____

_____

Frustrations:

_____

_____

_____

Decisions:

_____

_____

7 POWER MOVES to FINANCIAL FREEDOM

For use with *From Paychecks to Power*

LESSON 3: CHAPTER 2

It's Called "Personal Finance" for a Reason!

Lesson Focus: The focus of this lesson is defining personal finance and exploring the factors that contribute to an individual's financial situation.

Read *From Paychecks to Power*, pgs. 27-42

Financial Vocabulary: budgeting, saving, planning, forecasting, financial coach, debt, calculate, money, numbers game, math, relationships, environment, social/cultural practice, obligation, insurance, luxury, revenue, income, impulse buying, retail therapy, shop, retailer, trendy, intellect, wealth, financial principles, mortgage, physical condition, disability, slave, borrower, lender, informed consumer, uninformed consumer, negotiate, morals, values, principles, financial intelligence, rational mind, financial empowerment

Use one of the vocabulary activities on page 6 if you struggle to remember Financial Vocabulary meanings.

Borrower or Lender?

Place 8 vocabulary words from above in the box of either the borrower or the lender based on which is most applicable.

BORROWER	LENDER

> "Financial Freedom is not about how well you can calculate -
>
> it's about how well you personally behave!"
>
> **Shannaan Dawda**

Reflection:

What do you think the author means with this quote?

_____

_____

_____

_____

Managing your finances is about _____% math, _____% behavior, and _____% head knowledge.

Financial Influences:

What are the strongest influences on your finances? The author explains 7 areas that influence finances. List them in the order in which they influence your finances (1 - most influential, etc.).

1. _____

2. _____

3. _____

4. _____

5. _____

6. _____

7. _____

Give an example of how you have seen your top influencer in action.

_____

_____

_____

_____

Consumer Influences:

Go to a grocery or retail store and take note of how merchandisers get consumers to buy. Describe the display/influence and the resulting purchase they want you to make. Provide 4 examples.

Reflection:

What does this quote mean?   How does it apply to your current financial situation?

_____
_____
_____
_____
_____
_____

What Do You Stand For???

What do you stand for spiritually? Name 5 beliefs or values that describe you. Place one in each box below.

How do they influence your spending?

_____

_____

_____

_____

Principles or Feelings?

Create a graphic, design, or drawing that depicts the relationship between feelings and financial success.

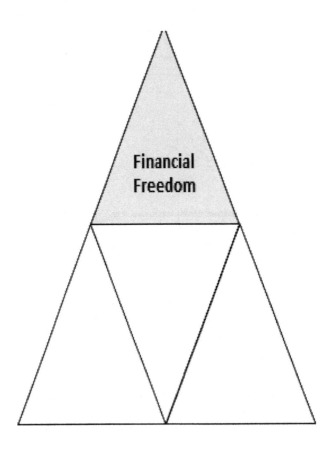

My Guiding Principles

The author states that the road to financial freedom must be based on principals rather than feelings. He cites Proverbs 22:7 as his guiding principle: "the borrower is slave to the lender".

List 1-3 principles you can stand on while you build financial freedom. Place them in the triangles below.

> *"Continue building and striving to live according to sound financial principles, and one day, you will be able to actually afford and maintain the luxury items you want – that is, if you still value them by then!"*
> **Shannaan Dawda**

Reflection:

What do you think the author means in the quote above? Why might your values change as a result of gaining financial freedom?

_____
_____
_____
_____
_____
_____
_____
_____
_____
_____

FROM PAYCHECKS TO POWER Journal Entry

Consider your current thoughts, practices, habits, and experiences related to this chapter. Record your thoughts about them as you think about your successes, reflections, successes, hangups, and resolutions

Reflections:

_____

_____

Successes:

_____

_____

_____

Frustrations:

_____

_____

_____

Decisions:

_____

_____

7 POWER MOVES *to* FINANCIAL FREEDOM

For use with *From Paychecks to Power*

LESSON 4: CHAPTER 3

Who Are You When It Comes to Managing Money?

Lesson Focus: The focus of this lesson is self-refection and discovery of how personality contributes to our viewpoints and practices in dealing with money.

Read *From Paychecks to Power*, pgs. 43-50

Financial Vocabulary: financial personality, saver, spender, frugal, nerd, free spirit

Use one of the vocabulary activities on page 6 if you struggle to remember Financial Vocabulary meanings.

Who Am I?

Place words that describe you touching the rings. The words closest to you should be descriptive of you with more intensity.

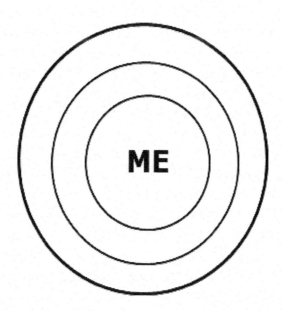

What is My Financial Personality?

Take the financial Personality Quiz below to find out...

Financial Personality Discovery Quiz:

The way in which you think about, relate to, and behave with your money says a lot about your Financial Personality! Everyone's Financial Personality is different; some are more prone to save, some are more prone to spend, and others fall somewhere in-between. Being aware of what your Financial Personality is will help you to be more conscious of your tendencies when it comes to dealing with money so that you can work to avoid the pitfalls that are most commonly associated with your particular personality. Thus, discovering what your Financial Personality is can be an illuminating and fundamental step on your journey to financial empowerment!

What is your Financial Personality? Answer the questions below, and then calculate your total score to find out!

1. Which of the following *first* comes to mind when you hear the word "budget"?

    a. Restrictions

    b. Control

    c. Responsibility

    d. Time-consuming exercise

2. When you receive extra money as a work bonus, gift, etc., what do you do with it?

    a. Spend it right away

    b. Put it in the bank

    c. Daydream about what you want to buy, but you ultimately save it

    d. Spend it, but change your mind several times on what you buy

3. If you were debt-free and had $1,000 with which you could do whatever you wanted, what would you do?

    a. Spend it before it hits the bank

    b. Invest it

    c. Buy a few small things or one semi-large purchase and save the rest

    d. Buy something that's been on your wish list for a while

4. How often do you go shopping (non-grocery related)?

    a. I shop frequently

    b. I only shop out of necessity

    c. I go once or twice a month but rarely buy anything

    d. I window shop and browse online often (at least weekly) but do not always buy

5. What would you do if your car broke down today and was deemed not repairable?

    a. I need a new car anyway, so I would find my way to a dealership

    b. Withdraw some money from my savings and buy a used car with cash

    c. Think that this a terrible tragedy and can't be happening

    d. Do research to find the lowest car payment to replace it

6. When is the last time that you had $1,000 in savings?

    a. I've never really attempted to save

    b. Now

    c. Within the last year

    d. Over a year ago

Scoring

In order to calculate your Total Score...

For every "a" answer, give yourself 5 points.

For every "b" answer, give yourself 2 points.

For every "c" answer, give yourself 4 points.

For every "d" answer, give yourself 3 points.

My Total Score: _____

Check Your Score

Use the Results Scale to determine your Financial Personality.

Results Scale

If your score is **25-30**, your Financial Personality is: **Complete Free Spirit!**

> **Assessment:** As a Free Spirit, you go with the flow of what you want to do with your money. You are more than likely easily pulled in by the latest sales, and you spend money freely… but all is *not* lost! The toughest part for you is doing a budget, because to you, a budget feels like something is restricting you – and Free Spirits like to run with the wind, not be restricted.

> **Challenge:** Change the way you see your budget! Rather than seeing it as a financial straitjacket that ties you down and restricts your movement, choose to see your budget as a plan that will help you get the things that you want while not jeopardizing your finances. Once you have become debt free, set aside a portion of your budget to freely spend however you like, Free Spirit!

If your total score is **19-24**, your Financial Personality is: **Free-spirited Nerd!**

Assessment: As a Free-Spirited Nerd, you still tend to go with the flow and do what you want with your money, but you tend to analyze and think twice about making purchases that cost more than a certain amount – an amount that you have established according to your financial comfort level. Consequently, though you may take those random shopping trips to the mall, you will not spend freely; it will be capped at a certain amount, and once you reach that amount, you're done – for now. It's the little spending here and there that keeps your finances in shambles, because each of these little spending incidents add up to a large amount of money that can be a big blow to your bank account!

Challenge: The fact that you are able to restrict your spending when it approaches a certain amount says that you have a financial conscience, which allows you to exercise a moderate level of discipline over your spending. Take things a step further by developing a budget and using this same discipline to keep you operating within its limits. When you become debt free, set aside a portion of your budget to spend on as many "little things" as you like. If you want to make a purchase that costs more than what you would normally spend, save up several pay periods' worth of money that you have budgeted for the little things and use them to make whatever big purchases you like – guilt free!

If your total score is **13-18**, your Financial Personality is: **Nerdy Free Spirit!**

Assessment: As a Nerdy Free Spirit, you like having a plan to keep your finances in order. While it is more than likely that you do not have a formal budget, the Nerd in you at least makes a half-hearted attempt to plan and regulate your spending by writing down your income and expenses on a piece of paper – or a napkin, or matchbook cover, or a sticky note – or you attempt to track your spending in your mind. However, sticking to such a non-concrete plan can be pretty tough for you, especially when the Free Spirit side of your financial personality kicks in!

Challenge: Don't kick yourself because you don't have the "formal budget thing" all together! The fact that you are making an effort to regulate your spending and that you are going through the exercise of charting your income versus your expenses for each pay period, regardless of where you might write them or how you mentally calculate them, says that you are committed to being financially responsible in your spending. As long as this is working for you – at least, for the most part – keep up the good work! You might go over in some areas of your budget, but as long as you meet your savings goals, you are good to go!

If your total score is **12**, your Financial Personality is: **Complete Nerd!**

Assessment: As a Complete Nerd, you have probably been budgeting since you were five years old! Okay, not really, but you probably have a massive, highly-detailed Excel spreadsheet that tracks your finances for the entire year. You save naturally, and spending money is rather difficult for you. In fact, spending money for you consists of nothing more than "splurging" for sushi night at your favorite spot. Other than that, you hold on to your money and gain greater pleasure from watching the balances of your accounts rise!

Challenge: Stick to your guns, and keep up the good work! Eventually, you will become debt free and start striving towards your larger financial goals, and this will empower you to live life on a whole other level! As you enjoy, yes please spend some of your money, your life of financial empowerment, be sure to take every opportunity to educate and empower others along the way so that one day, they can live financially empowered lives just like you!

My Financial Personality:

What is your financial personality? Did this surprise you? Why or why not?

_____
_____
_____

Why is it important to know yourself when planning for financial stability?

_____
_____
_____
_____

What characteristics do you recognize in financially successful people?

_____
_____
_____

$ Scenario: You just earned an unexpected $1000 beyond your regular pay working a one-time bonus job opportunity. What will you choose to do with it? Spend it, save it, or give it away?

Create a pie graph showing how you would spend, save, or give the money away.

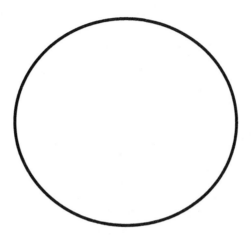

What does the above scenario illustrate about your financial personality? Is it consistent with your quiz results? Why or why not?

_____
_____
_____
_____
_____
_____
_____
_____

Family Influences

Think about 2 of your family members. Identify their financial personalities based on how they spend money.

Family Member #1: _____

Family Member #2: _____

How do you think their financial personalities have shaped your ideas of money, finances, and your resulting financial personality?

_____
_____
_____
_____
_____
_____
_____
_____

Family Tree

Look beyond the 2 family members you identified above. Create a Family Tree and note the financial personalities the best you can within your Family Tree.

FROM PAYCHECKS TO POWER Journal Entry

Consider your current thoughts, practices, habits, and experiences related to this chapter. Record your thoughts about them as you think about your successes, reflections, successes, hangups, and resolutions

Reflections:

_____

_____

Successes:

_____

_____

_____

Frustrations:

_____

_____

_____

Decisions:

_____

_____

7 POWER MOVES *to* FINANCIAL FREEDOM

For use with *From Paychecks to Power*

LESSON 5: CHAPTER 4

What's Your "Why"?

Lesson Focus: The focus of this lesson is to understand the motivation (the "why") of a person in pursuing financial freedom. Without knowing the "why" we do or want anything of true value, it is easier to fail. The sacrifices required can be too great unless we have a clear vision.

Read *From Paychecks to Power*, pgs. 51-56

Financial Vocabulary: motivation, sacrifice, success, freedom, income classes (lower, middle, high), options, mandates, habit(s), generational wealth, vision

Use one of the vocabulary activities on page 6 if you struggle to remember Financial Vocabulary meanings.

Financial Word Play:

Show the relationships between motivation, sacrifice, success, freedom, and habit in a visual format.

My "WHY":

What is your "why" for gaining financial freedom?

_____

_____

_____

_____

Illustrate your vision of financial freedom for yourself.

Sacrifice:

The author makes it clear that financial freedom requires sacrifice. What are you willing to give up to gain financial freedom?

_____
_____
_____
_____

Gaining financial freedom may mean you need to change some counter-productive habits. List 3 counter-productive habits that you recognize need to be broken and proactive habits you can replace them with to take you to financial freedom.

Counter-Productive Habits	Proactive Habits

> *"Champions keep going*
>
> *when there is nothing left in their tank."*
>
> **Shannaan Dawda**

Reflection:

How does this quote relate to working toward financial freedom?

_____
_____
_____

What do you think will be most challenging with working toward financial freedom? How do you plan to meet these challenges when you feel like giving up?

_____
_____
_____
_____
_____
_____

Create a Motto:

Create your own motto, saying, or slogan to help you to keep going when the journey to financial freedom seems too much to handle. Include your "why" as part of your motto.

Agree or Disagree?

Statement: *Our current entitlement society is oppressing the poor and insuring that they remain in poverty.*

Plan an argument for based on your beliefs about the statement above. Complete the web below with 3 main ideas and details that support your argument.

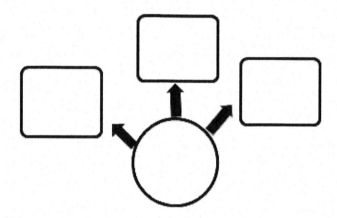

Impact of Beginnings:

Locate the Forbes list of the wealthiest Americans. Choose 2 who started from humble means. What did they do differently from others to achieve their success? Using 2 from humble means and 2 who were born into wealth, create a table to compare and contrast what those coming from humble means did differently from those who did not. Cite the traits that they possessed or developed that led to their success.

Person	Born into Humble Means or Wealth?	Characteristic 1	Characteristic 2	Characteristic 3

Do you think the "whys" of those born into wealth were different that those coming from a humble means? Why or why not?

_____
_____
_____
_____

FROM PAYCHECKS TO POWER Journal Entry

Consider your current thoughts, practices, habits, and experiences related to this chapter. Record your thoughts about them as you think about your successes, reflections, successes, hangups, and resolutions

Reflections:

_____

_____

Successes:

_____

_____

_____

Frustrations:

_____

_____

_____

Decisions:

_____

_____

7 POWER MOVES *to* FINANCIAL FREEDOM

For use with *From Paychecks to Power*

LESSON 6: CHAPTER 5

What's Your Financial Kryptonite?

Lesson Focus: The focus of this lesson is identifying and confronting that one thing in our lives that we enjoy owning, doing, or participating in that has the power to derail our progress toward financial freedom. Additionally, the secret and power of contentment is discussed.

Read *From Paychecks to Power*, pgs. 57-64

Financial Vocabulary: "financial kryptonite", cashier's check, impatience, contentment, acquisition, capitalize, best "bang" for your buck, prosper, anxiety

Use one of the vocabulary activities on page 6 if you struggle to remember Financial Vocabulary meanings.

Relationship between Impatience & Contentment

Illustrate the relationship between **financial kryptonite** and **contentment** below.

Power of Kryptonite:

The author described how his dream car, his financial kryptonite, almost destroyed his financial progress. Recall an experience or anticipate an experience that could easily prevent you from attaining financial freedom. Tell your story here: _____

_____
_____
_____
_____
_____
_____
_____
_____
_____
_____
_____
_____
_____
_____
_____
_____
_____
_____
_____
_____

Financial Kryptonite:

Draw a picture of yourself with your financial kryptonite. Label your financial kryptonite.

Avoiding the Kryptonite:

Name 3 things you can do proactively to avoid a kryptonite situation.

1. _____

2. _____

3. _____

Solution = Contentment:

What is contentment? _____
_____
_____
_____

How can you teach yourself contentment? _____
_____
_____
_____

Scenario:

Suppose that you are the columnist for a syndicated newspaper responsible for answering letters written to the column. You have received the following from a reader:

Dear Financial Coach: I've made such a mess of my life. No matter how hard I try, I don't seem to be able to get ahead. I've cut up my credit cards, but since I must have some way to get the items I need, I do carry some cash. Recently, I've been drawn to the shoe store around the corner from where I work. I already have 47 pairs of shoes, but every time I see the latest new styles, I can't contain myself. I purchase them, even if it means using money set aside for food and other bills. I've spent all the money set aside for food I had for this month on shoes and there are still two weeks left in the month, so I have no choice but to borrow money so I can eat. Can you help me?

Sincerely,
I Love Shoes

Compose a response for placement in your column containing the advice you would give to I Love Shoes. _____
_____
_____
_____
_____
_____
_____
_____
_____
_____
_____
_____

Most Common Culprits of Financial Breakdown:

Research the 10 items most frequently blamed for a financial breakdown. Display the list in priority order. Next to each, state a reason explaining why you believe this item is on the list.

Culprits of Financial Breakdown	Your Reason

FROM PAYCHECKS *TO* POWER **Journal Entry**

Consider your current thoughts, practices, habits, and experiences related to this chapter. Record your thoughts about them as you think about your successes, reflections, successes, hangups, and resolutions

Reflections:

_____

_____

Successes:

_____

_____

_____

Frustrations:

_____

_____

_____

Decisions:

_____

_____

7 POWER MOVES *to*
FINANCIAL FREEDOM

For use with *From Paychecks to Power*
LESSON 7: CHAPTER 6

The Credit Score Myth - EXPOSED!

Lesson Focus: Credit scores are widely misunderstood, and widely abused. The focus of this lesson is to dispel the myths and arm students with the tools they need to successfully navigate life, even absent a credit score.

Read *From Paychecks to Power*, pgs. 65-70

Financial Vocabulary: credit score, credit history, FICO, creditworthiness, wealth, afford, service account, deposit, payment, manual underwriting, mortgage

Use one of the vocabulary activities on page 6 if you struggle to remember Financial Vocabulary meanings.

Credit Score Myth:

Explain the credit score myth. Use 5 vocabulary words in your explanation.

_____
_____
_____
_____
_____
_____

Truth or Myth?   *"One must have credit or face a difficult life."*

Explain your answer. _____
_____
_____
_____

A FICO Score actually tells us _____.

FICO Social Profile:

Create a social media profile (Facebook Page, LinkedIn Profile, Twitter Profile, Instagram Profile, etc.) for FICO so others can get to know who he really is. Be sure to include information such as his date of birth, parents' names, etc., and feel free to add creative information to it.

Building a High FICO:

Why is building a high credit score actually counter-productive to becoming financially free?

_____
_____
_____
_____
_____
_____
_____

FICO Views:

Below are some credit scores. Write a plausible interpretation beside each score based on what you learned in this chapter.

Credit Score	Bank's View	Real Meaning
0		
560		
760		
480		

FICO Re-Focus:

Rather than focusing on maintaining a high credit score, what are 3 things you *should* focus on doing?

1. _____

2. _____

3. _____

According to the author, the BEST time to build credit is

_____.

Share the News!

The truth about credit is not taught to children often enough. Create a story board of a story you could tell a child to help him/her understand the credit myth.

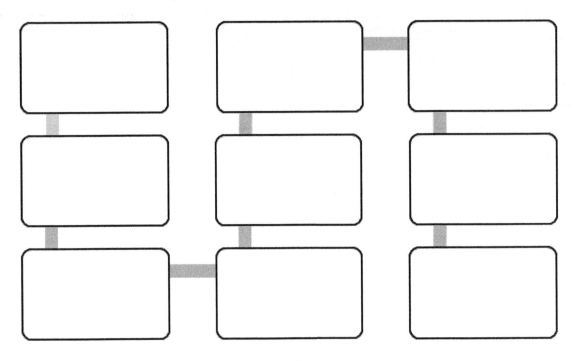

Illustrate one of the events from your story below:

FROM PAYCHECKS TO POWER Journal Entry

Consider your current thoughts, practices, habits, and experiences related to this chapter. Record your thoughts about them as you think about your successes, reflections, successes, hang-ups, and resolutions

Reflections:

_____

_____

_____

Successes:

_____

_____

_____

Frustrations:

_____

_____

_____

Decisions:

_____

_____

_____

7 POWER MOVES *to* FINANCIAL FREEDOM

For use with *From Paychecks to Power*

LESSON 8: CHAPTER 7

The Final Step before the Official Journey: Detoxing with a Financial Fast!

Lesson Focus: The focus of this lesson is preparation for changing habits related to dealing with money. The concept of a "financial fast" is introduced and readers are highly encouraged to participate.

Read *From Paychecks to Power*, pgs. 71-78

Financial Vocabulary: math, behavior, fast, financial fast, nickel & diming, financial empowerment, installments

Use one of the vocabulary activities on page 6 if you struggle to remember Financial Vocabulary meanings.

"Nickel & Diming":

List the small items that you purchase frequently that might be considered "nickel & diming" your finances. Place these items around the nickels and dimes below. Circle those items you purchase weekly or daily.

Explain how the nickel & diming concept and how it impacts finances.

_____

_____

_____

Financial Fast:

What is the purpose of the financial fast? Check all that apply.

_____ change spending habits   _____ do without necessities

_____ increase gratitude   _____ use credit card instead of cash

_____ lose weight   _____ save money

_____ fix a bad financial situation   _____ limit your income

What are 4 benefits of a financial fast?

Benefits of a Financial Fast			

List 10 free activities you can do during a financial fast rather than going out.

1. _____

2. _____

3. _____

4. _____

5. _____

6. _____

7. _____

8. _____

9. _____

10. _____

Budgeting for a Financial Fast:

Help a friend to use the budget on the next pages to prepare for a month of financial fasting, assuming his monthly income is $4,000/month.   Complete the budget for essential items.

Monthly Cash Flow Plan, aka "The Budget"

Monthly Cash Flow Plan

Cash flows in and out each month. Make sure you tell it where to go!

TRUE FINANCIAL
Real Financial Coaching, Real Financial Situations

Yes, this budget form has a lot of lines and blanks.

But that's okay. We do that so we can list practically every expense imaginable on this form to prevent you from forgetting something. Don't expect to put something on every line. Just use the ones that are relevant to your specific situation.

Step 1

Enter your monthly take-home pay in the box at the top right (**A**). This is the amount you have for the month to budget. So far so good, huh?

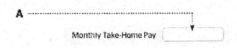

Step 2

Within each main category, such as Food, there are subcategories, like Groceries. Start at the top and work your way down, filling out the Budgeted column (**B**) first. Add up each subcategory and put that number in the Total box (**C**).

Also, pay attention to Dave's recommended percentages (**D**). This will help you keep from budgeting too much for a category.

Step 3

Finally, enter your take-home pay in the top box at the end of the page (**E**), then add up all categories and place that total in the Category Totals box (**F**). Then subtract your Category Totals amount from your Take-Home Pay. You should have a zero balance (**G**). Doesn't that feel great?

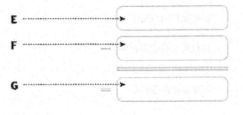

Step 4

When the month ends, put what you actually spent in the Spent column (**H**). That will help you make any necessary adjustments to the next month's budget.

Monthly Cash Flow Plan

Cash flows in and out each month. Make sure you tell it where to go!

TRUE FINANCIAL
Real Financial Coaching, Real Financial Solutions

Monthly Take-Home Pay [_____]

Add up budgeted column & enter here

These icons represent good options for cash envelopes

♥ CHARITY

	Spent	Budgeted
Tithes		
Charity & Offerings		
*10-15%		

🍎 FOOD

	Spent	Budgeted
✉ Groceries		
✉ Restaurants		
*5-15%		

🐷 SAVING

	Spent	Budgeted
Emergency Fund		
Retirement Fund		
College Fund		
*10-15%		

👕 CLOTHING

	Spent	Budgeted
✉ Adults		
✉ Children		
✉ Cleaning/Laundry		
*2-7%		

🏠 HOUSING

	Spent	Budgeted
First Mortgage/Rent		
Second Mortgage		
Real Estate Taxes		
Repairs/Maint.		
Association Dues		
*25-35%		

🚗 TRANSPORTATION

	Spent	Budgeted
Gas & Oil		
✉ Repairs & Tires		
License & Taxes		
Car Replacement		
Other _____		
*10-15%		

⚙ UTILITIES

	Spent	Budgeted
Electricity		
Gas		
Water		
Trash		
Phone/Mobile		
Internet		
Cable		
*5-10%		

🦷 MEDICAL/HEALTH

	Spent	Budgeted
Medications		
Doctor Bills		
Dentist		
Optometrist		
Vitamins		
Other _____		
Other _____		
*5-10%		

*Dave's Recommended Percentages

🛡 INSURANCE

	Spent	Budgeted
Life Insurance		
Health Insurance		
Homeowner/Renter		
Auto Insurance		
Disability Insurance		
Identity Theft		
Long-Term Care		
*10-25%		

👤 PERSONAL

	Spent	Budgeted
Child Care/Sitter		
Toiletries		
Cosmetics/Hair Care		
Education/Tuition		
Books/Supplies		
Child Support		
Alimony		
Subscriptions		
Organization Dues		
Gifts (inc. Christmas)		
Replace Furniture		
Pocket Money (His)		
Pocket Money (Hers)		
Baby Supplies		
Pet Supplies		
Music/Technology		
Miscellaneous		
Other _____		
Other _____		
*5-10%		

🏃 RECREATION

	Spent	Budgeted
Entertainment		
Vacation		
*5-10%		

🔑 DEBTS

	Spent	Budgeted
Car Payment 1		
Car Payment 2		
Credit Card 1 _____		
Credit Card 2 _____		
Credit Card 3 _____		
Credit Card 4 _____		
Credit Card 5 _____		
Student Loan 1		
Student Loan 2		
Student Loan 3		
Student Loan 4		
Other _____		
Other _____		
Other _____		
Other _____		
Other _____		

Your goal is 0% → *5-10%*

Once you have completed filling out each category,
subtract all category totals from your take-home pay.

Use the "income sources" form if necessary →

Add up totals from each category —

Remember—
The goal of a zero-based budget is to get this number to zero =

My Financial Fast Goals:

1. _____

2. _____

3. _____

Plan & Commit to a Financial Fast:

Why is it more impacting to only use cash during a financial fast?

_____

_____

_____

Financial Fast Dates: _____ to _____

Currency Use During Fast: ____ Credit ____ Debit ____ Cash

Fast Commitment Rating:

(1 = low commitment, 10 = high commitment)

| 1 | 2 | 3 | 4 | 5 | 6 | 7 | 8 | 9 | 10 |

←——————————————————————————————→

Explain the reason for your rating. _____
_____
_____

What are your top 3 concerns about this financial fast?

1. _____

2. _____

3. _____

FROM PAYCHECKS TO POWER Journal Entry

Consider your current thoughts, practices, habits, and experiences related to this chapter. Record your thoughts about them as you think about your successes, reflections, successes, hang-ups, and resolutions

Reflections:

_____

_____

Successes:

_____

_____

_____

Frustrations:

_____

_____

_____

Decisions:

_____

_____

7 POWER MOVES *to* FINANCIAL FREEDOM

For use with *From Paychecks to Power*
LESSON 9: POWER MOVE 1

Plan, then Command Your Money!

Lesson Focus: The focus of this lesson is understanding and developing a budget that takes into account the personality of the members of the household and establishes the basic guide to financial freedom.

Read *From Paychecks to Power*, pgs. 79-94

Financial Vocabulary: Power Move, command, money, govern, victim language, recipient, circumstances, proactive, intentional, budget, free-spending society, taboo, budget cuts, student loan, car payment, investing, eliminating, zero-based budget, accountability, attitude, behavior, desired outcome, spouse, healthy financial condition, team, budget meeting, understated, over-stated, The Nerd, The Free Spirit, marathon, sprint, budget plan, Murphy's Law, caveat

*Use one of the vocabulary activities on page 6 if you struggle to remember Financial Vocabulary meanings.

The Budget:

What are the first 3 words that pop into your mind at the mention of "budget"?

_____   _____   _____

Explain the differences between the **zero-based budget** and the **open-ended budget** in the T-chart below.

ZERO-BASED BUDGET   OPEN-ENDED BUDGET

💰 The KEY to POWER MOVE #1 is _____.

Steps to Establishing & Keeping a Budget:

1. Create the _____.

2. Focus ALL _____ on debt _____.

3. Enlist an _____ partner.

4. Schedule _____ budget _____.

Scenario:

You decide to establish a budget in order to trace your expenditures and focus extra monies on the debt you wish to pay off. Once your budget is established, you realize that with the high interest on your credit cards, you don't make enough every month to even pay all of your bills! What would you do? Explain your actions and reasoning below. _____
_____
_____
_____
_____
_____
_____
_____
_____
_____
_____
_____

Create Your Budget:

Create your monthly budget (for real) as you work to complete Power Move #1! Use the budget on the next few pages to help you with this task. Be sure to take into consideration both money personality types if you are doing this with a spouse.

Monthly Cash Flow Plan

Cash flows in and out each month. Make sure you tell it where to go!

TRUE FINANCIAL
Real Financial Coaching, Real Financial Situations

Yes, this budget form has a lot of lines and blanks.

But that's okay. We do that so we can list practically every expense imaginable on this form to prevent you from forgetting something. Don't expect to put something on every line. Just use the ones that are relevant to your specific situation.

Step 1

Enter your monthly take-home pay in the box at the top right (**A**). This is the amount you have for the month to budget. So far so good, huh?

Step 2

Within each main category, such as Food, there are subcategories, like Groceries. Start at the top and work your way down, filling out the Budgeted column (**B**) first. Add up each subcategory and put that number in the Total box (**C**).

Also, pay attention to Dave's recommended percentages (**D**). This will help you keep from budgeting too much for a category.

Step 3

Finally, enter your take-home pay in the top box at the end of the page (**E**), then add up all categories and place that total in the Category Totals box (**F**). Then subtract your Category Totals amount from your Take-Home Pay. You should have a zero balance (**G**). Doesn't that feel great?

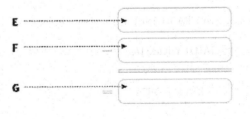

Step 4

When the month ends, put what you actually spent in the Spent column (**H**). That will help you make any necessary adjustments to the next month's budget.

Monthly Cash Flow Plan

Cash flows in and out each month. Make sure you tell it where to go!

Monthly Take-Home Pay [   ]

Add up budgeted column & enter here

These icons represent good options for cash envelopes

❤ CHARITY	Spent	Budgeted
Tithes		
Charity & Offerings		
*10-15%		

🍎 FOOD	Spent	Budgeted
Groceries		
Restaurants		
*5-15%		

🐷 SAVING	Spent	Budgeted
Emergency Fund		
Retirement Fund		
College Fund		
*10-15%		

👕 CLOTHING	Spent	Budgeted
Adults		
Children		
Cleaning/Laundry		
*2-7%		

🏠 HOUSING	Spent	Budgeted
First Mortgage/Rent		
Second Mortgage		
Real Estate Taxes		
Repairs/Maint.		
Association Dues		
*25-35%		

🚗 TRANSPORTATION	Spent	Budgeted
Gas & Oil		
Repairs & Tires		
License & Taxes		
Car Replacement		
Other _____		
*10-15%		

⚙ UTILITIES	Spent	Budgeted
Electricity		
Gas		
Water		
Trash		
Phone/Mobile		
Internet		
Cable		
*5-10%		

🩺 MEDICAL/HEALTH	Spent	Budgeted
Medications		
Doctor Bills		
Dentist		
Optometrist		
Vitamins		
Other _____		
Other _____		
*5-10%		

*Dave's Recommended Percentages

TRUE FINANCIAL
Real Financial Coaching, Real Financial Situations

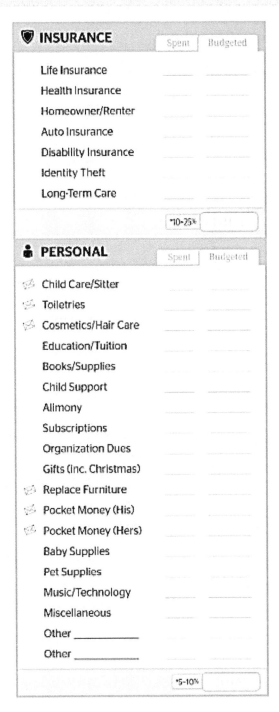

🛡 INSURANCE
	Spent	Budgeted
Life Insurance		
Health Insurance		
Homeowner/Renter		
Auto Insurance		
Disability Insurance		
Identity Theft		
Long-Term Care		
*10-25%		

👤 PERSONAL
	Spent	Budgeted
Child Care/Sitter		
Toiletries		
Cosmetics/Hair Care		
Education/Tuition		
Books/Supplies		
Child Support		
Alimony		
Subscriptions		
Organization Dues		
Gifts (inc. Christmas)		
Replace Furniture		
Pocket Money (His)		
Pocket Money (Hers)		
Baby Supplies		
Pet Supplies		
Music/Technology		
Miscellaneous		
Other _____		
Other _____		
*5-10%		

🏃 RECREATION
	Spent	Budgeted
Entertainment		
Vacation		
*5-10%		

🔑 DEBTS
	Spent	Budgeted
Car Payment 1		
Car Payment 2		
Credit Card 1 _____		
Credit Card 2 _____		
Credit Card 3 _____		
Credit Card 4 _____		
Credit Card 5 _____		
Student Loan 1		
Student Loan 2		
Student Loan 3		
Student Loan 4		
Other _____		
Other _____		
Other _____		
Other _____		
Other _____		

Your goal is 0% → *5-10%*

Once you have completed filling out each category, subtract all category totals from your take-home pay.

Use the "income sources" form if necessary

Add up totals from each category

Remember — The goal of a zero-based budget is to get this number to zero

Starter Emergency Fund:

What does the author suggest building a starter emergency fund before eliminating debt? Do you agree or disagree with this idea? Explain your thoughts.

_____
_____
_____
_____

Emergency Fund Uses:

The author defined what kinds of things constitute as "emergencies". Make a list of 5 possible uses for your Emergency Funds should they occur. Be sure to follow the author's guidelines.

1. _____
2. _____
3. _____
4. _____
5. _____

Planning & Commanding

You *command* your money only if you are _____ about what you do with it!

How long will it take you to build a starter emergency fund? _____

What amount will you be placing in it? _____

Who is your accountability partner? _____

When & where are your monthly budget meetings? _____

How much in resources will you put toward debt elimination each month? _____

FROM PAYCHECKS TO POWER Journal Entry

Consider your current thoughts, practices, habits, and experiences related to this chapter. Record your thoughts about them as you think about your successes, reflections, successes, hangups, and resolutions

Reflections:

_____

_____

Successes:

_____

_____

_____

Frustrations:

_____

_____

_____

Decisions:

_____

_____

7 POWER MOVES *to*
FINANCIAL FREEDOM

For use with *From Paychecks to Power*
LESSON 10: POWER MOVE 2

Get Your Snowball on a Roll!

Lesson Focus: This lesson focuses on an understanding of debt, attitudes related to debt, and eliminating debt through the debt snowball method.

Read *From Paychecks to Power*, pgs. 95-108

Financial Vocabulary: emergency starter fund, debt, debt-free, economist, economy, consumer, investor, debt-driven economy, debt-reduction, attitude, behavior, lifestyle, minimize, future gratification, spur-of-the-moment purchase, counterproductive, delayed gratification, broke, professional, pay off, interest rate, highest-to-lowest, outstanding debt, competitive, eliminate, paid-off, closed, debt consolidation, overspending, "debt snowball" method, debt balance, minimum monthly payment, collection agency, integrity, certified check, personal check, basic necessities

Use one of the vocabulary activities on page 6 if you struggle to remember Financial Vocabulary meanings.

The "Debt Snowball":

What is the "debt snowball" and how does it work? Explain it in your own words.

_____

_____

_____

Draw a picture to illustrate it.

Facing Debt:

T or F?

_____ 1. I am in debt because of your choices.

_____ 2. Debt is a symptom of overspending.

_____ 3. Attitude is everything!

Debt Reduction & Behavioral Changes:

Check the activities that may lead to debt reduction from the choices below.

_____ change in behavior   _____ change in lifestyle

_____ debt consolidation   _____ opening a new credit card

_____ making minimum payments   _____ frequent vacations

_____ spur of moment purchases   _____ delay pleasure

_____ separate needs from wants   _____ live on less than you make

_____ eating out often   _____ planning meals carefully

_____ evening bike ride   _____ game night at home

_____ night at the club   _____ frequent Starbuck's purchases

Anyone eliminating debt must make some behavioral changes, but for each of us these may be a little different. What 4 changes will you need to make in order to reduce debt?

1. _____

2. _____

3. _____

4. _____

💰 **The "debt snowball" method of eliminating debt is the most effective because it addresses the _____ that cause the _____!**

Getting Your Snowball to Roll:

Explain the 3 steps you will take to get *your* "debt snowball" on a roll.

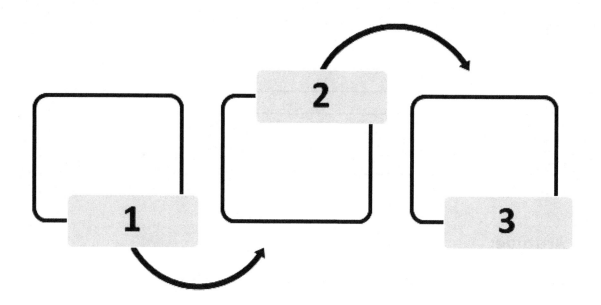

My Debts:

List your debts here as you think of them. Then number them in the order they should be paid according to the "debt snowball" method.

Payoff Order	Debt	Debt Amount
TOTAL DEBT		

Integrity & Attitude:

What do "integrity" and "attitude" have to do with financial matters?

_____
_____
_____
_____
_____

Give an example from your own life.

_____
_____
_____
_____
_____

Coaching Notes:

The author notes 3 tips at the end of this chapter. List them here.

Tip #1	Tip #2	Tip #3

Your "WHY" is extremely important in this Power Move...why?

_____
_____
_____

What was your most powerful "take-away" from this chapter? Why?

_____
_____
_____

FROM PAYCHECKS TO POWER Journal Entry

Consider your current thoughts, practices, habits, and experiences related to this chapter. Record your thoughts about them as you think about your successes, reflections, successes, hang-ups, and resolutions

Reflections:

_____

_____

Successes:

_____

_____

_____

Frustrations:

_____

_____

_____

Decisions:

_____

_____

7 POWER MOVES *to* FINANCIAL FREEDOM

For use with *From Paychecks to Power*

LESSON 11: POWER MOVE 3

Take the Urgency Out of Emergency!

Lesson Focus: This lesson focuses first on building an adequate emergency fund, then on guidelines for purchasing a home.

Read *From Paychecks to Power*, pgs. 109-120

Financial Vocabulary: celebrate, debt-free, milestone, debt-strapped, emergency fund, fully-funded, employment, return on money, growth of money, accessible, replenish, dream home, price point, investment property, renter, mortgage, down payment, private mortgage insurance (PMI), premium, beneficiary, retirement, college fund, underfunded, real estate bubble, foreclosure

Use one of the vocabulary activities on page 6 if you struggle to remember Financial Vocabulary meanings.

Celebrate a Milestone!!

Being debt-free is something to celebrate! Illustrate your planned celebration when you are debt-free.

Fully Funding an Emergency Fund:

My fully funded emergency fund covers ___ months of household expenses.

Uses for my emergncy fund:

_____

My monthly expenses =

_____

If not yet funded, I will put _____ toward it until I reach the total amount needed.

My emegency fund will be placed in:

_____

Total amount saved for my emergency fund: _____

Home Buying:

What 2 things should be in place BEFORE you buy a home?

_____   _____

Draw and label your **DREAM HOME**:

Make a Case for Your Home Purchase:

Choose a house currently for sale that you think you can afford if the 2 criteria above have been met and you continue to earn the money you currently earn.

Describe the house here:

_____
_____
_____
_____

Why do you think you can afford this home?

Reasons I Can Afford This Home	

How do you plan to purchase this home (length of mortgage, money down, etc.)?

_____
_____
_____
_____

When do you plan to pay it off?

_____

What is the author's guideline for a monthly house payment? Why is this important, even if you are debt free?

_____
_____
_____
_____
_____
_____

Mortgage Guidelines:

List 3 mortgage guidelines the author suggests if you need to get a home mortgage.

Guideline #1	Guideline #2	Guideline #3

Foreclosures:

Research the damage foreclosures can have to your finances. Draw a graphic to show how this information.

Home Buying Goals:

Based on the information you learned in this chapter, what are your home buying goals? State 2 goals you have in this area using estimated time frames and dollar amounts.

1. _____

2. _____

FROM PAYCHECKS TO POWER Journal Entry

Consider your current thoughts, practices, habits, and experiences related to this chapter. Record your thoughts about them as you think about your successes, reflections, successes, hang-ups, and resolutions

Reflections:

_____

_____

Successes:

_____

_____

_____

Frustrations:

_____

_____

_____

Decisions:

_____

_____

7 POWER MOVES *to* FINANCIAL FREEDOM

For use with *From Paychecks to Power*

LESSON 12: POWER MOVE 4

Invest Today for a Comfortable Tomorrow!

Lesson Focus: The focus of this lesson is an understanding of how to save and invest for the later years of life.

Read *From Paychecks to Power*, pgs. 121-130

Financial Vocabulary: invest, nest egg, foresight, wisdom, capacity, desire, reverse mortgage, sustainability, resources, legacy, consumer debt, Dow Jones Industrial average (the Dow), percent, assumption, pre-tax, 401k, 403b, individual retirement account (IRA), Roth, tax benefit, tax code, Social Security, for-profit, non-profit, matching contributions, withdrawal, corporate ladder, lock in rate, tax bracket, stock, mutual fund, shares, company, stock market, fluctuation, portfolio, industry, balanced portfolio, international market, yield, diversify

Use one of the vocabulary activities on page 6 if you struggle to remember Financial Vocabulary meanings.

Investment Vocabulary:

Choose 3 of the investment vocabulary words above to explain in your own words.

1. [   ] _____

2. [   ] _____

3. [   ] _____

To invest is to _____ _____.

Building a Legacy:

There are many reasons people invest their money or build wealth. What are your primary reasons for investing?

_____
_____
_____

What does it mean to "build a legacy"? How do you envision that for yourself and your family?

_____
_____
_____
_____
_____
_____

Write a mission statement to guide your investment strategy. Remember, mission statements are usually 1-2 sentences long, and succinctly state your core beliefs.

_____
_____
_____
_____

> The author asserts that "the power of focusing on the right things at the right times, determines how much we get done and how effectively".

Reflection:

_____
_____
_____
_____

Retirement:

How much is enough when saving for retirement?

_____

_____

_____

Why is it wise to build a "nest egg" when you are young?

_____

_____

_____

Investment Power:

The author suggests investing _____% of your income at as early an age as possible. If you are debt-free, this is very simple.

If you started investing the suggested amount at your current salary with 9% interest, how much would you be investing each month? _____

If you kept this investment consistent for 30 years, how much money would you earn?

_____

Play the Stock Market:

Choose 3 stocks and 3 mutual funds to research. Look at their growth over the past year and over the past ten years. Create a chart to show which stock or mutual fund you believe to be the best for you.

Simulation:

Pretend you have $10,000 of money to invest in the stock market. "Spend" your money on stocks and track any growth or decline over a specified period of time. (The minumum time required for this activity is 1 week.) Collect your stock purchases at the beginning of the activity and complete a daily status check along the way. Complete a table or graph illustrating your stock's progress.

Name 2 things you learned from working with stocks:

1. _____

2. _____

The IRA:

Use a Venn Diagram to compare a Traditional IRA to a Roth IRA.

Traditional   **Roth**

Which type of IRA is best for you and why?

_____
_____
_____

Stocks vs. Mutual Funds:

You have $10,000 to put toward stocks or mutual funds. Which would you choose and why? State your choice: _____ and 3 reasons for your decision.

1. _____

2. _____

3. _____

Investment Decisions:

Choose one of the scenarios below and complete the suggested activity to show your understanding of investment strategy.

Scenario #1

You are 25 years old and have just become debt free. At your income level of $45,000, you can comfortably invest $6,750 (15% of $45,000) annually. Given that your income is increasing by 3% a year and that you maintain your investment contribution at 15%, how much will you have in your retirement savings at age 65 if the annual interest rate you earn on that money averages a modest 5% a year? Show this example in a digital brochure add promoting investing.

Scenario #2

You've just started your dream job, working for a great company. You've completed your probationary period and are now being asked to enroll for company benefits. As you read the materials in preparation for meeting with the enrollment counselor, you notice that you will need to determine what percentage of your income to invest in the company's 401k plan.   You can also choose, or decline matching funds up to a certain level. Assume you make $65,000 gross a year and the company match tops out at $4000 in a year. You are debt free, so no worries there. What percentage should you invest? Should you accept the company offer? Explain how you arrived at your conclusions by creating a digital presentation outlining the scenario and the reasoning for your conclusion.

Balanced Portfolio:

Draw an example of a balanced investment portfolio in the space below.

Social Security:

Research the answers to these questions about Social Security & record 1 new thing you learn from your research:

- Do you have to be retired to get Social Security? How old must you be?

- Is there any advantage to waiting until a later age to draw Social Security?

- What exactly is Social Security?

New Thing: _____

My Investment Goals:

Outline your investment goals below based on your current salary. If you need to become debt free first, calculate when you will be able to begin investing.

Annual Investment Money: _____

Start Time: _____

Investment Strategy:

_____

_____

_____

_____

The Best Advice:

What were the 3 best pieces of investing advice you gained from the author?

Advice #1	Advice #2	Advice #3

Hind Sight:

Knowing what you know now, what would you have done earlier in your life & why?

_____

_____

_____

FROM PAYCHECKS *TO* POWER Journal Entry

Consider your current thoughts, practices, habits, and experiences related to this chapter. Record your thoughts about them as you think about your successes, reflections, successes, hangups, and resolutions

Reflections:

_____

_____

Successes:

_____

_____

_____

Frustrations:

_____

_____

_____

Decisions:

_____

_____

7 POWER MOVES *to* FINANCIAL FREEDOM

For use with *From Paychecks to Power*

LESSON 13: POWER MOVE 5

Eliminate the Fees from Your Kids' Degrees!

Lesson Focus: The focus of this lesson is to explore different types of college savings plans and to explain the benefits of setting starting these types of plans early in order to remove one type of debt that future generations often face.

Read *From Paychecks to Power*, pgs. 131-136

Financial Vocabulary: student loan debt, milestone, generation, graduation, debt load, proactive, financial stability, special education investment account, savings bond, ROI (Return on Investment), 529 Plan, Education Savings Account (ESA), after-tax, tax-free, tuition, room and board, qualified education, contribution, penalties, private school, vocational school

Use one of the vocabulary activities on page 6 if you struggle to remember Financial Vocabulary meanings.

A Basket Full of Bricks:

How are student loans like a basket of bricks to the college graduates launching to get a first jobs in their careers? Use 4 vocabulary words in your answer.

_____

_____

_____

Staggering Facts:

\[$\] _____% of college graduates have student loan debt

💵 The average loan balance is _____!

> **"Student loans are the roadblock of this generation of students."**
>
> **Rachel Cruze**

Reflection:

_____

_____

Name 3 things student loan debt can keep graduates from being able to do?

1. _____

2. _____

3. _____

ESA vs. 529 Plans:

Use the T-chart to state benefits of each of these plans for saving for a child's college education.

ESA Plan	529 Plan

Which plan would you most likely use to save money for your child's education?

_____

If you started saving when your child was born, how much would you need to invest each month, according to the author? _____

Did this surprise you? Why or why not?

_____

_____

_____

Scenario #1:

You started saving for your child's education when he was born, but when he was 3 years old, you experienced a divorce and loss of income. To make ends meet as a single parent, you stopped the monthly investment. When your son was 10 years old, you remarried and were able to continue investing at the same rate of $150/month. What should you do to be sure there is enough college money set aside by the time your son turns 18 years old?

_____

_____

_____

_____

Scenario #2:

Devon is planning to start college at age 25 after working for Best Buy for 6 years. His parents were not able to put money aside for college for him and they have encouraged him to "work his way through college" as they had done. What advice would you give to Devon as he plans to work and go to school in order to finance college for himself?

_____

_____

_____

Scenario #3:

Charisse and Jim have just had their first child. Collectively, they make $45,000/year. They are eager to start saving for their child's education even though things are tight financially. They still have $20,000 of debt to pay off in order to be debt free. What would you suggest they do: pay their debt first, pay down their debt and start saving, or ignore their debt and start saving instead?

_____

_____

_____

My Goals for College Savings:

Share your goals for saving for the education of your children.

_____

_____

_____

FROM PAYCHECKS *TO* POWER Journal Entry

Consider your current thoughts, practices, habits, and experiences related to this chapter. Record your thoughts about them as you think about your successes, reflections, successes, hang-ups, and resolutions

Reflections:

_____

_____

Successes:

_____

_____

_____

Frustrations:

_____

_____

_____

Decisions:

_____

_____

7 POWER MOVES to FINANCIAL FREEDOM

For use with *From Paychecks to Power*

LESSON 14: POWER MOVE 6

Make Your House a Home, Not a Prison!

Lesson Focus: The focus of this lesson is strategies for gaining true financial freedom by paying off a mortgage, thereby owning the home in which you live.

Read *From Paychecks to Power*, pgs. 137-140

Financial Vocabulary: homestead, imprisoned, house poor, home ownership, mortgage, rent, asset, investment, terms of mortgage, stipulate, fixed rate mortgage, ARM, discretionary income, mortgage payment, pay off, net worth, lease, rental contract

Use one of the vocabulary activities on page 6 if you struggle to remember Financial Vocabulary meanings.

"House Poor"?

What does it mean to be "house poor"?

_____

_____

_____

_____

_____

How can you avoid becoming "house poor"?

_____

_____

_____

_____

_____

Benefits of Home Ownership (Mortgage Free):

List some benefits of owning your home mortgage free:

Benefits of Owning a Home without a Mortgage	

Goal of Home Ownership:

According to the author, what should the goal of home ownership really be? _____

_____

_____

Mortgages:

Research the difference in final total payback for a mortgage of $250,000 using a 15 year mortgage as compared to a 30 year mortgage. Show the comparison in the graphic.

15 Year Fixed

30 Year Fixed

Types of Mortgages:

There are other types of mortgages beyond the 15 and 30 year fixed. Investigate the traditional, jumbo, and the ARM mortgages. Complete the web below with details of each mortgage type.

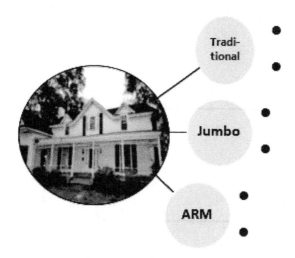

Rent or Buy?

How do you know if it is smarter to rent or buy? Research the monthly cost of renting a 3 bedroom/2 bathroom home in your area. Explain how this compares to the total of the anticipated payment on a 15 year fixed rate mortgage and monthly expenses for a home of similar size, location, and type in your community.

_____

_____

_____

_____

_____

_____

_____

_____

Scenario:

Determine how much house a family of four making $75,000 a year should be able to afford. They have just become debt free and have funded a starter emergency fund. Window shop for a house to agree with their needs and budget. Establish the mortgage terms and down payment and calculate when they should buy and how long it would take them to pay off a 15 year mortgage. Present your calculations in a PowerPoint, but outline your slides here:

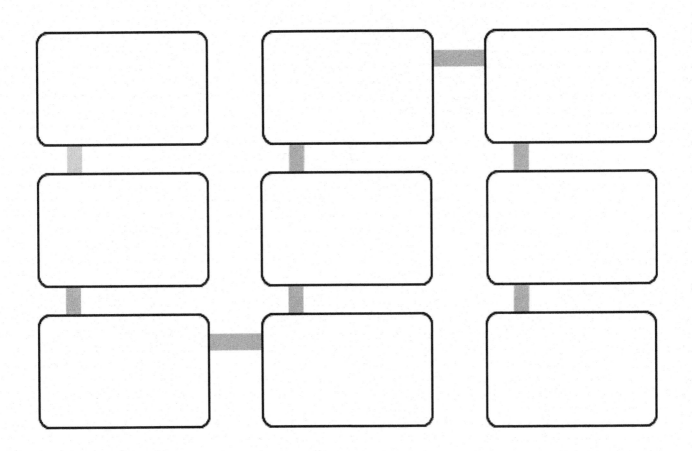

FROM *PAYCHECKS* TO POWER Journal Entry

Consider your current thoughts, practices, habits, and experiences related to this chapter. Record your thoughts about them as you think about your successes, reflections, successes, hang-ups, and resolutions

Reflections:

_____

_____

Successes:

_____

_____

_____

Frustrations:

_____

_____

_____

Decisions:

_____

_____

7 POWER MOVES *to* FINANCIAL FREEDOM

For use with *From Paychecks to Power*

LESSON 15: POWER MOVE 7

More Money - More Options to Give & Live!

Lesson Focus: The focus of this lesson is what to do with your money once you've achieved financial freedom through eliminating debt, fully funding retirement, emergency and college funds, and paying off your house. Specifically charitable donations, increasing retirement contributions, sharing some of your wealth with family and enjoying the purchase of some of the items you desire are discussed.

Read *From Paychecks to Power*, pgs. 141-144

Financial Vocabulary: options, ambitions, desires, dreams, retirement goals, retirement calculator, charitable donation, compassion, selfish, maturity, cash-flow

Use one of the vocabulary activities on page 6 if you struggle to remember Financial Vocabulary meanings.

Vocabulary Highlights:

Choose 3 vocabulary words to highlight by using each in a financial context.

1. ☐ _____

_____

2. ☐ _____

_____

3. ☐ _____

_____

True or False?

_____ 1. Anyone is able to live a debt-free life if they exercise discipline and maturity in the handling of their finances.

_____ 2. Giving benefits the giver as much as it benefits the receiver.

_____ 3. It takes maturity to become debt-free.

Choose one of the statements above to explain in detail, whether it is true or false, and why. Include an example if possible.

_____
_____
_____

Revisiting Retirement Goals:

The author advises revisiting retirement goals once you are debt free.

Revisiting Retirement Goals	How much are you currently contributing toward retirement?	
	Use a retirement calculator (online) to determine what you will have to live on in retirement. Amount to live on for retirement:	
	Are you on target to live the lifestyle you desire when you retire?	
	What is your monthly income goal for retirement?	
	If not, how much should you add to your monthly contribution to get there?	

Revisited Retirement Action Plan:

_____
_____
_____
_____
_____

Why Give?

The author states that we are managers of what our Creator places in front of us. Our direction is to (in specific order)...

Giving strengthens and builds positive _____ in our lives, the **most important thing in life**!

My Giving Plan:

Once you are completely debt free, how do you believe you will spend your money? Are there causes, places of worship, or other charitable organizations you desire to support? Are there family members who need your help? Plan your giving by placing the receivers in the appropriate boxes. Larger boxes symbolize more money going to those people/organizations while smaller boxes represent small amounts to others. Feel free to add boxes of various sizes if needed.

Choose one of the planned recipients of your giving above and explain your reason for wanting to give to that person or organization. _____
_____
_____
_____

Eliminating Debt:

By eliminating debt from your life, what are some things (dreams, passions, etc.) YOU are positioning yourself to do? Place one dream or passion in each thought cloud.

Spending Plan:

Once you are debt-free and have completed your Giving Plan, you will be spending money! Create a Spending Plan based on your dreams and passions above. Plan your giving by placing the receivers in the appropriate boxes. Larger boxes symbolize more money spent while smaller boxes represent small amounts to spend. Feel free to add boxes of various sizes if needed.

A Life Free from Financial Stress:

In the text, the author states that "the kind of life each of us was created to live" is "a life free of financial stress". Based on the text, how would you describe a "life free of financial stress"? Draw an illustration to promote your points.

Decisions:

1. If you are able, is there ever a time that it is okay to refuse to help someone who has a need? Debate this with someone close to you and express your thoughts here: _____
_____
_____
_____
_____
_____

2. Research a charitable entity to which you would like to be able to contribute. Specifically, how much the organization's revenue actually goes to the cause and what percent goes to overhead and administrative costs? Complete the pie graph showing this information.

Name of Charitable Organization:

Would this influence your giving to the organization? How?

_____
_____
_____

FROM PAYCHECKS TO POWER Journal Entry

Consider your current thoughts, practices, habits, and experiences related to this chapter. Record your thoughts about them as you think about your successes, reflections, successes, hangups, and resolutions

Reflections:

_____

_____

Successes:

_____

_____

_____

Frustrations:

_____

_____

_____

Decisions:

_____

_____

7 POWER MOVES *to* FINANCIAL FREEDOM

For use with *From Paychecks to Power*

LESSON 16: BONUS CHAPTER

Common Personal Finance Myths - EXPOSED!

Lesson Focus: The focus of this lesson is to expose the truth concerning three of the most common myths concerning money and finance.

Read *From Paychecks to Power*, pgs. 145-148

Financial Vocabulary: myth, reward points, credit card, freebies, swipe, percentage fee, merchant, retailer, balance, cash back program, market ploy, debit card, PIN, receipt, fraudulent, write-off, mortgage interest, APR

Use one of the vocabulary activities on page 6 if you struggle to remember Financial Vocabulary meanings.

True or False?

_____ 1. Credit cards are a great way to pay for purchases because they have lots of safety features built in, like fraud protection.

_____ 2. It is better to have mortgage when it comes to tax time so that you have the home mortgage deduction.

_____ 3. Using your debit card as a debit card is safer than running it as a credit card.

Lure of Reward Points:

Explain how reward points work for credit card use. Are these points actually "free"? Is there ever an appropriate time to use a credit card? Explain. _____
_____
_____
_____

Credit or Debit?

Write a blog post of 250 words or less explaining the best way to use a debit card. _____
_____
_____
_____
_____
_____
_____
_____
_____
_____
_____
_____

Marketing Ploys:

Identify a specific credit or retail marketing ploy that encourages credit card use. Analyze the benefits to the retail store and credit card company and list them below. Identify the benefits to the consumer as well. Who really "wins"?

Marketing Ploy: _____

Benefits to Retail Store and/or Credit Card Company	Benefits to the Consumer

Tweet a Warning:

Explain in a tweet (140 characters or less) how credit card companies make money. _____

_____

_____

_____

Scenario #1:

Your best friend is all excited about reward points from her credit card that she can use to pay for some specific items, even though she admits that the items she sees in the catalogue are not items she would purchase otherwise. She is sure this is "free money". She wants to know why you aren't using the same card. As a matter of fact she can get bonus points for getting you to apply for the same card if you are accepted. How will you respond to her request to submit your name? Why will you answer as you did? _____

_____

_____

_____

_____

Scenario #2:

You are a credit counselor and a pair of roommates has just entered your office seeking professional help to take control of their credit card help. Here is there debt record:

- MasterCard 1: $2512 balance, minimum payment of $90, 4.5% interest rate

- Visa 1: $4000 balance, minimum payment of $100, 9% interest rate

- Department Store Credit Card: $516 balance, minimum payment of $15, 27% interest rate

- MasterCard 2: $7400 balance, minimum payment of $125, 19% interest

Using the "debt snowball" method, prepare a budget for paying off this debt given that the roommates have a budget of $400 a month for debt reduction.

What advice will you give them to help them to stay out of debt once paid?

_____

_____

_____

Scenario #3:

Your new job requires travel. While you are able to use a company credit card most of the time to secure hotel rooms and rental cars, there are occasions when you plan an extra day or two prior to your work nights to visit friends or family. You do not have your own credit card since you wish to remain debt-free. How can you travel without one of your own? Research some options and choose the best one for you. Explain what you would do.

_____

_____

_____

_____

My Intentional Response (action plan) to 3 myths in this chapter:

MYTH   **My Plans to Avoid the Traps**

1
-
-

2
-
-

3
-
-

FROM PAYCHECKS TO POWER Journal Entry

Consider your current thoughts, practices, habits, and experiences related to this chapter. Record your thoughts about them as you think about your successes, reflections, successes, hangups, and resolutions

Reflections:

_____

_____

Successes:

_____

_____

_____

Frustrations:

_____

_____

_____

Decisions:

_____

_____

7 POWER MOVES *to* FINANCIAL FREEDOM

For use with *From Paychecks to Power*

LESSON 17: PERSONAL FINANCE WRAP-UP

What Does It Mean for Me?

Lesson Focus: The focus of this section is to bring everything together, a type of review.

Read *From Paychecks to Power*, pgs. - Review Various Chapters

Financial Vocabulary: caveat, money, Murphy's Law, sales tax, income tax, state income tax, levy, debt snowball

Use one of the vocabulary activities on page 6 if you struggle to remember Financial Vocabulary meanings.

Taxes:

We've only briefly talked about taxes. It has been stated that there are two certainties in life, death and taxes. It seems like taxes are everywhere. Research the taxes that are unique to your locality and state. List them here along with their rate if it is available. Examples include sales tax, state income tax, etc.

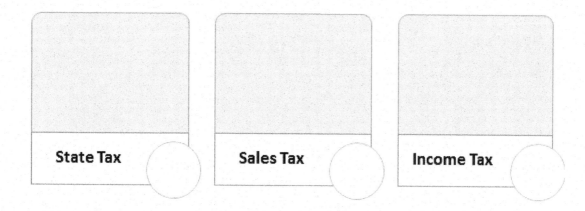

State Income Tax:

Research which states have state income tax. There actually are only a few that do not. Which do not? Why do states levy state income tax anyway? Explain your findings in a graphic illustration.

Debate a Concept:

Choose one of the following to statements. Determine & state your stance or point of view. (agree or disagree).   Then list at least 3 reasons to support your point.

1. A sticking to a budget is a very liberating activity.

2. It is possible to live without debt.

Concept:	

What is the real goal of money?

How do you answer this question now? Have your ideas changes?

_____

_____

_____

_____

Budgeting:

By now, you should have established a budget. What is the goal of budgeting? How can it really help? Draw a short cartoon that illustrates the goal of budgeting and why it is important.

Importance of Accountability:

How do I stay on track to meet my goal? Great question, and one that speaks to accountability. In addition to getting an accountability partner as referenced earlier, there are many ways to track your own decision-making and actions.

Identify Your Areas of Concern: _____

Research an app that can help you to stay accountable. Feature it here with an advertisement.

FROM PAYCHECKS TO POWER Journal Entry

Consider your current thoughts, practices, habits, and experiences related to this chapter. Record your thoughts about them as you think about your successes, reflections, successes, hang-ups, and resolutions

Reflections:

_____

_____

Successes:

_____

_____

_____

Frustrations:

_____

_____

_____

Decisions:

_____

_____

7 POWER MOVES *to*
FINANCIAL FREEDOM

For use with *From Paychecks to Power*
LESSON 18: NEXT STEPS

Now What?

Lesson Focus: The focus of this lesson is to review and ensure that participants are ready to move forward after the completion of the course.

Read *From Paychecks to Power*, pgs. Review Various Chapters

Financial Vocabulary: juncture, momentum, financial kryptonite, goal, investment plan, fixed benefit plan, mortgage, tax deduction, Social Security

Use one of the vocabulary activities on page 6 if you struggle to remember Financial Vocabulary meanings.

Addressing Your Financial Kryptonite:

Recall the discussion on "financial kryptonite"? Do you remember what yours was? Take a peek back to Lesson 7 if you can't recall what it was. Is it still an issue for you? If so, confront it now and resolve to overcome. Create a 4 step plan to dissolve it.

My Next Steps to Financial Freedom:

You've actually arrived at one of the hardest junctures in this course. Summarize your learning and create your next steps concerning how you plan to keep your momentum toward financial freedom going over time. This can be completed on the next page.

My Next Steps to Financial Freedom:

What were the KEY elements learned in *From Paycheck to Power?* What next steps will YOU take in breaking negative cycles in your life?

What I Knew	What I Learned	Baby Steps to Reach Success	End Goal (Success)

My Support Group:

Who is your support group? List them here.

1. _____

2. _____

3. _____

4. _____

When It Gets Tough:

What will you do when the going gets rough?

_____

_____

_____

_____

Rate Yourself:

The author states that making changes takes hard work. Rate your **desire** for change, as well as your **level of commitment** to the work required to make this change. Place an "X" on each continuum below that reflects your desire and level of commitment to this process. Look back to the first lesson...have your desire and level of commitment changed?

Little Desire ⟵————————————⟶ **High Desire**

Low Commitment ⟵————————————⟶ **High Commitment**

Built-In Support:

The road to financial freedom is sometimes very long. The 7 Power Moves Checklist can support you along the way to help you know if you are applying the principles found in this book in your everyday life. Utilize the 7 Power Moves Checklist (p. 113) and Rubric (p. 114) to track your progress in moving toward financial freedom with your daily habits. As your behaviors change, it will get easier and easier to move to financial freedom...and stay there.

FROM PAYCHECKS *TO* POWER Journal Entry

Consider your current thoughts, practices, habits, and experiences related to this chapter. Record your thoughts about them as you think about your successes, reflections, successes, hang-ups, and resolutions

Reflections:

_____

_____

Successes:

_____

_____

_____

Frustrations:

_____

_____

_____

Decisions:

_____

_____

FROM PAYCHECKS *TO* POWER
Post Test

What do you know about money and financial literacy? Do your best to complete each question. A pre/post assessment is a good way to review a book. It will give you an idea of how much information you have gained.

1. The wealthiest nation in the world is:

    a.   China

    b.   Iran

    c.   United States of America

    d.   Germany

2. The path to financial excellence/wealth is

    a. Finding the right investment to grow my investment quickly

    b.   Hard work and discipline

    c.   Meeting the right people and making the right connections

    d.   Making the right deal

3. The best way to "get rich quick" is

    a.   Find the right deal

    b.   Borrow money to invest in a high yield account

    c.   Don't

    d.   Participate in a Nigerian scheme

4. Debt takes a toll on _____.

    a.   Your ability to set-up an emergency fund

    b.   Relationships

    c.   Your health

    d.   All of the above

5. Financial freedom is essentially about

    a.   Writing a budget

    b.   Personal behavior

    c.   Calculating your expenses properly (Doing the math)

    d.   How much money you make

6. Most Americans

    a.   Have adequate funds in the bank to handle emergencies

    b.   Live paycheck to paycheck

    c.   Teach their children good financial habits through example

    d.   Teach their children good financial habits intentionally

7. Personal finance is about

    a.   How you handle your money

    b.   Preparing a budget

    c.   Managing your credit card balances properly

    d.   Maintaining a good credit score

8. A borrower is

    a.   Able to get what he wants when he wants it

    b.   To be admired for his ability to get more credit

    c.   Helping the economy by spending money

    d.   A slave to the lender

9. The two major types of financial personalities are

    a.   Saver and Spender

    b.   Frugal and Spendthrift

    c.   Free Spirit and Nerd

    d.   Not easily defined

10. In planning a budget, it is important to know

    a.   What your parents thought about money

    b.   Your debt tolerance

    c.   Your Credit Score

    d.   Your financial personality

11. In order to make the sacrifices required for financial freedom, it is important to know the

    a.   Why

    b.   Amount

    c.   Bank Rate

    d.   Your Credit Score

12. Knowing why you are seeking financial freedom makes it easier to

    a.   Fail

    b.   Give up

    c.   Compromise

    d.   Keep going even when it gets tough

13. Our "financial kryptonite" is that one thing that

    a.   Keeps us focused on the goal

    b.   Derails our financial progress

    c.   Gives us real power

    d.   Enables us to get the goods we want now

14. Much advertising is based on

    a.   Appealing to our need to overcome low self-concept and self-image

    b.   A sincere desire to keep us well informed

    c.   Good intentions in helping us spend our money wisely

    d.   Keeping us up to date and current

15. Your credit score tells a lender

    a.   Whether you can afford to make the payments required

    b.   How good you are at borrowing money and paying it back

    c.   Whether you manage your money well or not

    d.   Whether you are a good provider for your family

16. Obtaining a mortgage to buy a house while not having a credit score, because you don't have a credit history, requires you to

    a.   Build your credit first, so you have an extensive credit history

    b.   Just accept that you can't afford to get a house

    c.   Undergo "Manual Underwriting"

    d.   Rely on friends or family to underwrite your mortgage

17. Which of the following are impossible to accomplish without a credit score

    a.   Get a mobile (cell) phone account

    b.   Buying a car

    c.   Getting a job where the prospective employer pulls your credit history

    d.   None of these, all are possible without a Credit Score

18. Statistically, when someone pays for items with cash they

    a.   Spend less

    b.   Spend more

    c.   Spend the same

    d.   Are happier with their purchase

19. One long-time, widely accepted, and highly successful method of budgeting is to use

    a.   Credit cards, but always pay them off

    b.   An envelope system and cash

    c.   Separate checking accounts

    d.   Your memory to inform you of whether a purchase is in your budget or not.

20. Being proactive means you are _____.

    a.   For everything

    b.   Exercise regularly

    c.   Fight hard for what is right

    d.   Intentional in your actions

21. A budget is

    a.   A tool used to achieve financial freedom

    b.   Denying access to things

    c.   Impossible to follow

    d.   By its very nature restrictive and difficult to stick to

22. Which type of budgeting is best for most people?

    a.   Open-Ended Budgeting

    b.   Zero-Based Budgeting

    c.   Both are equally beneficial for everyone

    d.   Neither, they are too restrictive

23. Household monthly budget meetings are necessary for

    a.   Reporting

    b.   Accountability

    c.   Maintenance of the budget

    d.   All of the above

24. Having a budget allows you to _____ your money.

    a.   Command

    b.   Spend

    c.   Save

    d.   Increase

25. Debt consolidation is not an effective way to get out of debt because

    a.   It doesn't get you out of owing the debt

    b.   The debt consolidator is the only one making money

    c.   It only treats the symptoms of the debt issue, not the cause

    d.   This is a false statement, because it is an effective solution

26. In using the "Debt Snowball" Method of getting out of debt, which would you pay first?

    a.   The debt with the lowest interest rate

    b.   The debt with the highest interest rate

    c.   The debt with the lowest balance

    d.   The debt with the highest balance

27. Integrity is

    a.   Being honest

    b.   Honoring your word

    c.   Having strong moral values

    d.   All of the above

28. What are the first bills that should be paid each month?

    a.   Clothing, food, transportation, insurance

    b.   Food, utilities, shelter, transportation

    c.   Food, cell phone, transportation, student loans

    d.   Credit cards, rent, food, clothes

29. A fully funded Emergency Fund will include how many months' worth of expenses

    a.   three to six

    b.   one to three

    c.   six to nine

    d.   nine to twelve

30. What is the recommended minimum down payment when purchasing a house?

    a.   5 percent

    b.   10 percent

    c.   20 percent

    d.   25 percent

31. If you must use a mortgage to buy a house, what is the recommended maximum term?

    a.   15-Year

    b.   20-year

    c.   30-Year

    d.   40-Year

32. What is the maximum percentage of your take home pay that should be allocated to a house payment in order for the payment to be considered affordable?

    a.   10

    b.   20

    c.   25

    d.   50

33. As a general rule of thumb, how much of your income should you invest?

    a.   15% of your take home from the very first paycheck

    b.   15% of your gross income from your very first paycheck

    c.   15% of your gross income, but only after you are debt-free and have a fully funded emergency-fund

    d.   Any excess income after paying your expenses

34. Practically speaking, the best retirement savings accounts are

    a.   Traditional IRAs, there is a reason they've been around a long time

    b.   Roth IRAs, these will grow tax free because you've already paid the taxes upfront

    c.   Savings Bonds

    d.   Bank Certificate of Deposits

35. Paying off your house using your discretionary income

    a.   Is a bad idea, because it eliminates the tax write off of mortgage interest

    b.   Is okay if you really want to

    c.   Puts you in the best position to build wealth

    d.   Just doesn't make sense, discretionary income is just for having fun and taking vacations

36. Someone who becomes debt-free by budgeting and managing their money becomes

    a.   financially powerful

    b.   financially responsible

    c.   financially independent

    d.   all of the above

7 POWER MOVES Checklist

How are my financial habits growing?

Check all that apply today.

PLANNING & COMMANDING

☐ Establish a budget

☐ Utilize Debt Snowball method to eliminate existing debt

☐ Establish an emergency fund

☐ Recognize my kryptonite Participate in a financial fast

☐ Track my spending habits

☐ Reward myself at milestones

BUILDING SAVINGS

☐ Put money aside from every paycheck

☐ Build small emergency fund before eliminating debt

☐ Fully fund emergency fund after eliminating debt

☐ Build retirement funds

☐ Eliminate all debt

☐ Start college funding when children are born

☐ Pay off my home

☐ Invest

MAKING WISE DECISIONS

- ☐ Distinguish between needs and wants prior to purchasing
- ☐ Avoid using credit
- ☐ Avoid my kryptonite
- ☐ Meet with an accountability partner regularly
- ☐ Give to others
- ☐ Know my financial personality
- ☐ Set goals & stick to them
- ☐ Learn contentment
- ☐ Follow my budget
- ☐ Prioritize my bills monthly

7 Power Moves Daily Score: __ / 25 _____ %

7 POWER MOVES Rubric:

Participant Name: _____

Date: _____

Daily/Weekly Goal: _____

1 – made **very few or no** wise financial moves today

2 – made **a few** wise financial moves today

3 – displayed **several** wise financial moves today

4 – displayed **many** wise financial moves today

Complete and initial the Self Rating (S). Two ratings per day are available for use.

Teacher/Period	Monday	Tuesday	Wednesday	Thursday	Friday	Total
Self	1 2 3 4	1 2 3 4	1 2 3 4	1 2 3 4	1 2 3 4	
	1 2 3 4	1 2 3 4	1 2 3 4	1 2 3 4	1 2 3 4	
Self	1 2 3 4	1 2 3 4	1 2 3 4	1 2 3 4	1 2 3 4	
	1 2 3 4	1 2 3 4	1 2 3 4	1 2 3 4	1 2 3 4	
Self	1 2 3 4	1 2 3 4	1 2 3 4	1 2 3 4	1 2 3 4	
	1 2 3 4	1 2 3 4	1 2 3 4	1 2 3 4	1 2 3 4	
Self	1 2 3 4	1 2 3 4	1 2 3 4	1 2 3 4	1 2 3 4	
	1 2 3 4	1 2 3 4	1 2 3 4	1 2 3 4	1 2 3 4	
Self	1 2 3 4	1 2 3 4	1 2 3 4	1 2 3 4	1 2 3 4	
	1 2 3 4	1 2 3 4	1 2 3 4	1 2 3 4	1 2 3 4	
Self	1 2 3 4	1 2 3 4	1 2 3 4	1 2 3 4	1 2 3 4	
	1 2 3 4	1 2 3 4	1 2 3 4	1 2 3 4	1 2 3 4	

My Reflections on the Week: _____

Participant Signature: _____

College & Career Readiness Checklist

Readiness Area	Skill	Completed	Notes
Core Content	Academic requirements met		
	Career & technical education standards met		
College & Career Pathways	Educational aspirations		
	Eligibility for educational aspirations met		
	Career exploration		
	Career aspirations		
Demonstrated Social & Emotional Skills	Self-management skills		
	Responsible decision-making skills		
	Self-awareness skills		
	Social awareness skills		
	Relationship skills		
Demonstrated Higher-Order Thinking Skills	Problem-solving skills		
	Synthesis & precision skills		
	Critical thinking & reasoning skills		
Demonstrated Academic Success & Employability Skills	Inquisitiveness & intellectual openness		
	Organization & study skills		
	Research skills		
	Attendance		
	Engagement to tasks		
	Teamwork & collaboration		
	Effective communication skills		
Demonstrated Civic/Consumer/Life Skills	Civic management		
	Financial literacy & management		
	Information technology		
	Social media skills		
Completed Products	Resume		
	Job applications		
	College applications		
	Letters of recommendation		
	Cover letter		
	FAFSA		
	Budget/Financial Plan		
	7 Power Moves Portfolio		

From Paychecks to Power & the *7 Power Moves Participant Portfolio* taught me many things that have helped me to prepare for college and/or my career. Three (3) ways the book prepared me for college and/or career are:

1. _____

2. _____

3. _____

My primary goal as a result of this preparation is...

_____

_____

_____

_____

FROM PAYCHECKS TO POWER

Pre / Post Test Answer Key

1.	c.	19.	b.
2.	b.	20.	d.
3.	c.	21.	a.
4.	d.	22.	b.
5.	b.	23.	d.
6.	b.	24.	a.
7.	a.	25.	c.
8.	d.	26.	c.
9.	a.	27.	d.
10.	d.	28.	b.
11.	a.	29.	a.
12.	d.	30.	c.
13.	b.	31.	a.
14.	a.	32.	c.
15.	b.	33.	c.
16.	c.	34.	b.
17.	d.	35.	c.
18.	a.	36.	d.

CPSIA information can be obtained
at www.ICGtesting.com
Printed in the USA
BVOW09s1045190217
476594BV00013B/132/P